...ΙΕΒΟΑΙ...
ΟΤΕ ΧΕΣ
ΥΣΙΧΣ
ΡΙΣΤΟΛΕΝΡ
ΟΙ ΝΟΣ
ΝΟΤΙΜΟΣ
ΛΛΟΝΙΧΕΣ
ΑΛΙΧΣ ΕΝΟ
ΕΙΝΙ Σ
ΕΜΙΚΧΟΟΣ
ΙΜΟΔΕΜΟΣ
ΥΣΙΣ
ΚΕΣΙΑΣ
ΠΙΧΑΒΕΣ

The Louvre

Greek, Etruscan and Roman Antiquities

Alain Pasquier

EDITIONS
SCALA

Réunion des musées nationaux

© 1991 Scala Publications Ltd.
Published by Editions Scala
14 bis, rue Berbier-du-Mets - 75013 Paris

Cover : *The Victory of Samothrace*

CONTENTS

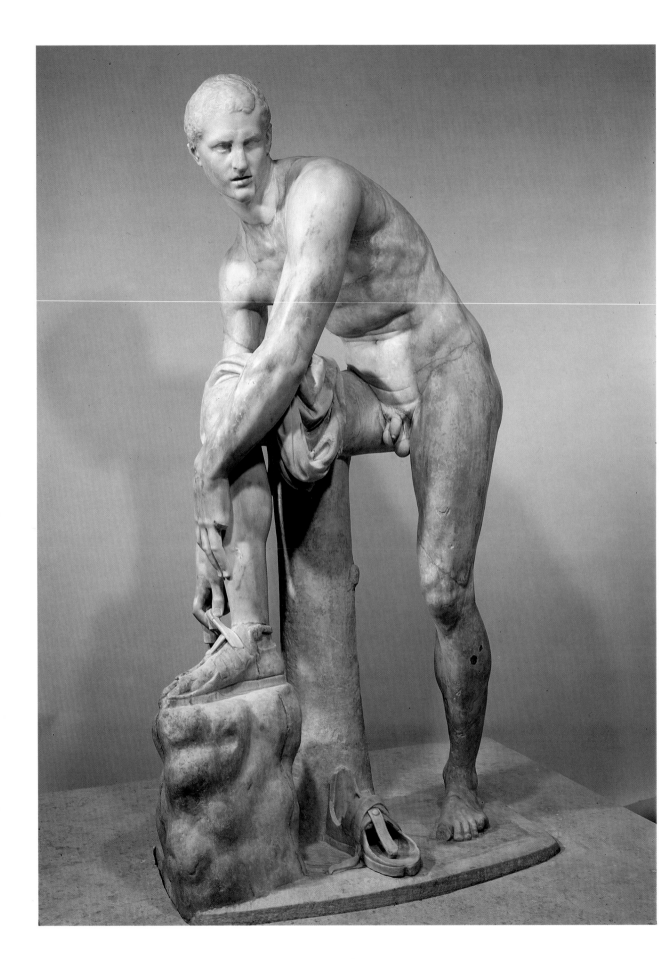

HISTORY OF
THE DEPARTMENT

The Department of Greek, Etruscan and Roman Antiquities is one of the oldest departments of the Louvre. Indeed, from the time of the Legislative Assembly's decree creating the Muséum Central des Arts on 16th September, 1792, a part of the Palace was devoted to the presentation of antiquities. This was the "Petite Galerie", the summer apartments of the Queens of France, with ceilings painted by Romanelli and his workshop. Several plans were drafted; but it was only in 1800 that the First Consul opened the Musée des Antiques, with a very different arrangement from that envisaged at the beginning of the project. The prizes of war seized by General Bonaparte in his victories in Italy suddenly increased both the quantity and the quality of the collections assembled round the old royal collection. The triumphal procession of 10th Thermidor, Year 6 (29th July, 1798) included very many famous sculptures surrendered by the Treaty of Tolentino in 1797 : the Laocoon group, the Apollo Belvedere, the Dying Gaul, the Venus de' Medici, amongst others. Enthusiasm for the antique, stimulated by the discovery of Herculaneum and Pompeii and set in order by the theories of Winckelmann, saw these very objects as the peak of art, and they were placed at the critical points of the exhibition. Vivant Denon was director of the Musée, while Ennius Quirinus Visconti, who had fled from Italy, had come to supervise the Greek and Roman antiquities. The newly arrived works were very distinguished; but those which had been seized by the Revolutionaries and brought together in Paris were also of very high quality. There was a core formed by the collections of the King, which included certain statues that had been there since the reign of François I. A collection of great interest was created by adding the marbles belonging to two great men, Cardinal Richelieu and Cardinal Mazarin, who both imitated the Renaissance Popes in their avid and enthusiastic collecting of antiquities. The Kings of France had bought the *Diana with the Faun*, the *Venus Genetrix* and the *Germanicus* (renamed *Marcellus*) signed by Cleomenes, and to these were added statues like the *Wounded Amazon* from Richelieu's collection and the *Apollo Citharoedus* from Mazarin's collection, as well as many other ancient stones which adorned their sumptuous residences. The basic appearance of the ancient sculpture at the Muséum was already being changed by confiscations from Italian collections, such as those of the Albani and Braschi families. (Compensation for the latter was to come in 1802.) An upheaval occurred in 1808, however, when Napoleon enriched the Muséum by purchasing the Borghese Collection from his brother-in-law, Camille Borghese, which added several hundred pieces to the existing collection. The *Gladiator*, the *Hermaphrodite*, and the bust of *Homer* entered the Louvre, as well as a group of Roman sarcophagi of the highest quality. They were to stay there, unlike many other pieces that the armies of the Revolution and then of the Empire had accumulated at Paris. Their intention had been to carry out the Convention's plan to form the greatest museum ever in the capital of France and of Liberty; but these ambitions and hopes came to an end with the fall of the Empire and the abdication of Napoleon I.

After the Congress of Vienna the sculptor Canova organised the restitution of what had been confiscated, subject to certain arrangements made with Vivant Denon, which allowed the Louvre, now the Musée Royal, to keep works as important as the *Tiber* and the *Sarcophagus of the Muses*. Certain pieces were too difficult and too dangerous to transport back, and this simplified the negotiations. These quite proper restitutions created some gaps, and the areas where the ancient sculpture was exhibited were extended; but in spite of this illustrations of the exhibition show how many sculptures and reliefs were to be seen in the galleries and how densely they were packed.

The Emperor's successors regarded it as their duty to enrich the ancient collections. During this period of the Restoration many works from the Albani Collection and then from the Choiseul-Gouffier Collection, including the metope from the Parthenon, were restored to their owners, but were then properly acquired. This shows particularly well that there was a continuity in the acquisitions policy, and it is to the credit of the Kings of France that they had the political wit not to question it. The most important event, however, was the arrival of the *Venus de Milo*. It was given to Louis XVIII by the Marquis de Rivière, who sent it immediately to the Louvre, in accordance with the wishes of the donor. The arrival of the Tochon Collection, in 1848, led to the registration of 574 vases and the beginning of the Greek pottery section, which was destined to have a brilliant future. Under Charles X the marbles collection was augmented by fragments of the very important decoration of the Temple of Zeus at Olympia, the most important pre-classical Greek monument, discovered by a scientific expedition to the Morea. They were parts of several metopes from its Doric frieze. The Greek National Assembly, which met at Argos in 1829, gave them to France in recognition of her part in the struggle against Ottoman rule. Small objects such as bronzes, vases and terracottas began to increase in number in 1825, with the purchase of the Chevalier Edme-Antoine Durand's first collection, joined in 1836 by part of the second collection immediately put together by this indefatigable collector of antiquities. These were the first signs of an interest which was to grow and which was in particular to give the Louvre one of the finest collections of ancient vases in the world. The reign of Louis-Philippe saw the acquisition of the *Piombino Apollo*, a bronze statue found in the sea; but it also saw the strengthening of a phenomenon already represented by the arrival of the Olympia marbles, the growth of the ancient collections of the Musée Royal by means of scientific expeditions, or by the personal action of diplomats of every rank who were in post in countries where the classical civilisations had flourished. This is how the reliefs of the Temple of Athena at Assos found their way to the Louvre, given by the Sultan Mahmoud, and how the friezes of the Temple of Artemis Leucophryene, from Magnesia on the Maeander, joined them a little later, thanks to the enterprising Charles Texier. Sixty-nine metres of relief, with the traditional theme of the Amazonomachy, were entered in the museum's inventories, giving it a particularly fine example of the architectural sculpture of the Hellenistic period. This is also how Commandant Delamare's mission to North Africa added greatly to the Roman monuments with a large number of tombstones, inscriptions and statues.

The accession of Napoleon III was an important date in the history of the Department. Not only were the ancient galleries thoroughly renovated, but they received some acquisitions of the highest importance. Of the marbles mention must be made of the *Victory of Samothrace*, sent by Charles de Champoiseau, France's Consul at Adrianople. This, the Louvre's monumental beacon, arrived at Paris in several consignments of fragments; but when restored it was to occupy a place of honour at the top of the staircase in the Pavillon Daru. It was also Champoiseau who found the two torsos of kouroi at Actium and sent them to Paris. The reliefs of the *Passage of the Theores*, from the island of Thasos, were acquired thanks to the Miller expedition, as were the sculptured pillars of an enigmatic Roman building at Salonica, to which popular imagination in the Middle Ages had given the Spanish name of "Incantada", or enchanted palace. Finally, mention must be made of the *Stele of Pharsalos*, brought back by the Léon Huzzey expedition.

The most considerable acquisitions during the Second Empire, however, were the big assemblages of small objects. Vattier de Bourville sent not only a group of fine marbles from Benghazi, but also several hundred vases and terracotta statuettes from Cyrenaica. Archaic Greek pottery and figurines came from the Salzmann Collection, which was formed from excavations carried out in Rhodes. Ernest Renan's expedition to Phoenicia led to the Louvre acquiring such notable antiquities as the mosaic pavement from the *Church of Saint Christopher of Qabr-Hiram*, near Tyre in the Lebanon. All that, however, is nothing compared with the purchase of the extraordinary, massive collection of the Marquis Campana. Its arrival at the Louvre brought about a profound change in all areas of the Department, and made the Louvre the greatest museum in the world, both in the quantity and in the quality of its Greek and Etruscan vases. The excavations carried out by the Italian collector's orders, principally on the site of the Etruscan cemetery of Cerveteri, north of Rome, brought an enormous mass of objects to light, as from others. They ranged from the most modest little jugs to the ambitious *sarcophagus* of a man and wife, an absolute masterpiece of Etruscan art. Although there was considerable argument about this fabulous acquisition, both during the negotiations and after their conclusion, the impact it produced can be judged from the fact that there were thousands of pottery vessels (about 3,500, including the undecorated vessels), and an important group of big statues, the superb fragment of the *Ara Pacis*, and a considerable number of bronze and terracotta figurines.

After 1870 it is again the growth of the collection of small objects, particularly the terracotta statuettes, which is worth mentioning. Figurines from the tombs excavated at Tanagra, which is the neighbouring site to Thebes in Boeotia, were acquired on the initiative of Olivier Rayet, while others were acquired in the gifts of P. Gaudin. The latter included the famous group of five hundred well-preserved statuettes excavated in the cemetery of Myrina in Asia Minor, which were very representative of the small-scale sculpture of the Hellenistic period. By the beginning of the Second Republic, however, the period of great acquisitions had passed. The countries of the ancient civilisations were formulating stricter and more efficient legislation to prevent the departure of works found in their soil. But a few outstanding acquisitions were to enhance the Louvre's collection from time to time, such as the *Kore of Samos*, sent by Paul Girard, or the head of the *Rider*, bequeathed by Georges Rampin, and it is round these that the important fragments of the first period of Greek sculpture are grouped today.

The end of the 19th century was particularly fortunate for this section of the Louvre. Patronage was now responsible for the arrival of élite objects, and it too raised the quality of the whole. Gustave and Edmond de Rothschild offered the Louvre the marbles found at Didyma, at Heraclea under Latmos and at Miletus, which consisted of fragments of architecture, inscriptions and statues, brought to light by the excavations of O. Rayet and A. Thomas. They included the enormous column-bases from the Temple of Apollo at Didyma and a monumental male torso, which show very clearly the transition from Archaic to Classical art. Some time later the same donors most generously sent to the Louvre the greater part of the large hoard of Roman silver plate which had been found in a villa at Boscoreale, near Pompeii. They thus inspired others who had acquired objects from the same treasure to become donors and to make the museum's holding of such antiquities one of the richest in the world.

Photographs taken at the end of the century show that the Department's galleries of sculptures and of smaller objects were excessively overloaded. Almost everything was on exhibition, with a mixture of periods and styles, and it was not well arranged. The First World War, when the collections had to be put away in store, was the opportunity for a reorganization which was only completed in 1936. The collections were enhanced by the arrival of the "*Dame d'Auxerre*", which was exchanged for a picture handed over to the town's museum, and by the finds from excavations at Eleon in the Dardanelles, carried out by French soldiers under the direction of members of the French School at Athens. With these additions the collections were re-exhibited in a brighter and more spacious part of the museum. Many objects were put away in the reserves, while those that were kept in the galleries began to be put out in a chronological sequence, in order to demonstrate one aspect or another of Greek, Etruscan or Roman art. As far as sculpture is concerned, this is the period when the authorities of the museum began a campaign to remove restorations from the marbles. Ancient fragments of good quality, but burdened with modern artificial limbs which had no archaeological or aesthetic purpose, were freed from their inopportune grafts. Purchases continued, but at a more moderate pace and more sporadically. The acquisition of important mosaic pavements from the Franco-American excavations at Antioch-on-the-Orontes, in Turkey, must be mentioned again here. In accordance with the agreement between the local authorities and the participants eleven mosaics were given to the Louvre, and they form the finest collection of pavements from the Near East outside their country of origin. Nearer home, the collection of glass and small bronzes was augmented by the De Clercq-Boisgelin gift, including some pieces of first-class quality.

Since 1970 there has scarcely been a year when the Department has not brought into the museum objects which complete a series, or introduced a new category not previously represented in the collections. Examples are the colossal bronze head of the Emperor Hadrian, which is a masterly addition to the already impressive collection of imperial portraits, or the Campanian bell-krater attributed to the Ixion Painter. Its ambitious decoration doubtless recalls a great lost painting, the *Massacre of the Suitors by Odysseus and Telemachus*. An important recent event which will long be remembered is the gift of the two last silver vessels from the Boscoreale Treasure which remained in the Rothschild Collection. They are decorated with historical scenes, and they complete the museum's picture of this luxury tableware.

The Departmental curators always remember that one of their duties is the enrichment of the collections; but their principal task during the current renovation of the Louvre is the reorganization of the exhibitions. In the ground-floor galleries the sculpture has been reorganised in a less mannered presentation, with more neutral bases, more sober backgrounds, more informative labels, and particularly with artificial lighting to replace or reinforce the sometimes rather sparse daylight. A task still remaining on this floor is the organization of a supplementary area given to the Department as a result of the "Grand Louvre" project, the gallery bordering the north side of the Visconti Courtyard, under the Daru Gallery. The reorganization of the first-floor galleries includes such important operations as the remounting of the bronzes gallery, the creation of a silver gallery and of another for ancient glass, and lastly the refurbishment of the Greek vase gallery (the Campana Gallery), enlarged with part of the Musée Charles X. These plans are the main projects which the curators are currently planning and putting into effect.

GREECE

0   100 km

ADRIATIC SEA

MAGNA GRAECIA
Paestum
Tarentum

IONIAN SEA

SICILY
Agrigento
Gela
Syracuse

MACEDONIA
Pella

THRACE
Byzantium

Thasos
Samothrace

PHRYGIA
Troy
Assos

Corcyra
Dodona

THESSALY
Sesklo
Dimini

AEGEAN SEA

Cyzicus

Pergamum
Myrina

Ithaca
Delphi
Thebes
BOEOTIA
ATTICA
Athens
Corinth
Mycenae
Piraeus
Olympia
Argos
Aegina
Sparta
Epidaurus

Clazomenae
Ephesus
Samos
Delos
Miletus
CYCLADES
Paros
Naxos

CARIA
Halicarnassus
Cos
LYCIA

Pylos

Melos
Thera

Xanthos
RHODES

Knossos
Mallia
Phaistos
CRETE

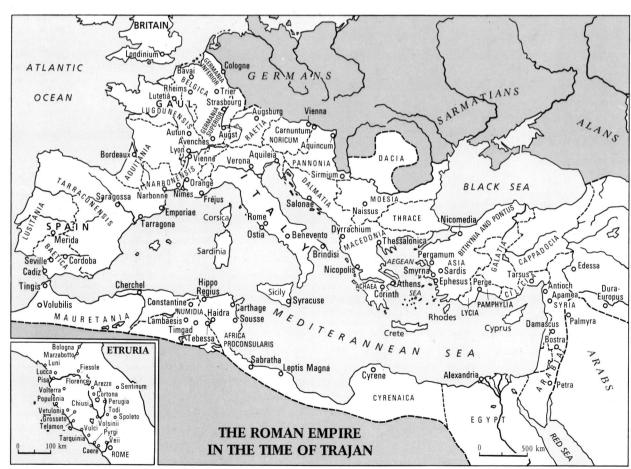

**THE ROMAN EMPIRE
IN THE TIME OF TRAJAN**

0   500 km

BRITAIN
Londinium

ATLANTIC OCEAN

Bavai
GERMANIA INFERIOR
Cologne
GERMANS
BELGICA
Rheims
Trier
Lutetia
GAUL
Strasbourg
LUGDUNENSIS
Augsburg
Vienna
SARMATIANS
ALANS
Autun
GERMANIA SUPERIOR
Augst
RAETIA
Carnuntum
NORICUM
Aquincum
Avenches
Lyon
AQUITANIA
Vienne
Aquileia
Verona
PANNONIA
DACIA
Bordeaux
Sirmium
Orange
NARBONENSIS
DALMATIA
BLACK SEA
Saragossa
Narbonne
Nimes
Fréjus
MOESIA
TARRACONENSIS
Emporiae
Corsica
Rome
Salonae
Naissus
Nicomedia
SPAIN
Tarragona
Ostia
Benevento
Dyrrachium
THRACE
BITHYNIA AND PONTUS
LUSITANIA
Merida
Sardinia
Brindisi
MACEDONIA
Thessalonica
Pergamum
ASIA
GALATIA
CAPPADOCIA
Edessa
BAETICA
Cordoba
Nicopolis
Smyrna
Sardis
Tarsus
Seville
AEGEAN
Antioch
Dura-Europus
Cadiz
Sicily
Syracuse
ACHAEA
Athens
Ephesus
Perge
CILICIA
Apamea
Tingis
Cherchel
Hippo Regius
Constantine
Corinth
SEA
PAMPHYLIA
SYRIA
Volubilis
NUMIDIA
Haidra
Carthage
LYCIA
Rhodes
Cyprus
Damascus
Palmyra
MAURETANIA
Lambaesis
Timgad
Tebessa
Sousse
Bostra
AFRICA PROCONSULARIS
Crete
MEDITERRANEAN SEA
ARABIA
ARABS
Sabratha
Leptis Magna
Cyrene
Alexandria
Petra
CYRENAICA
EGYPT
RED SEA

ETRURIA

0   100 km

Bologna
Marzabotto
Luni
Fiesole
Lucca
Pisa
Arezzo
Florence
Volterra
Sentinum
Cortona
Populonia
Perugia
Chiusi
Vetulonia
Todi
Spoleto
Grosseto
Volsinii
Telamon
Vulci
Tarquinia
Pyrgi
Veii
Caere
ROME

CHRONOLOGY

GREECE

NEOLITHIC PERIOD	**before 3200 BC**
BRONZE AGE	**about 3200-1200 BC**
Early bronze	3200-2000 BC
Middle bronze	2000-1580 BC
Late bronze	1580-1200 BC
DARK AGE	**1200-1050 BC**
IRON AGE	**1050-end of 1st millennium BC**
Protogeometric period	1050-900 BC
Geometric period	900-720 BC
Orientalizing period	720-620 BC
Archaic period	620-480 BC
Early classical period	480-450 BC
Classical period	450-330 BC
Hellenistic period	330-30 BC

ETRURIA

Villanovan period	900-700 BC
Orientalizing period	700-580 BC
Archaic period	580-470 BC
Classical period	470-330 BC
Hellenistic period	330-1st century BC

ROME

REPUBLIC	**509-27 BC**
EMPIRE	**27 BC-395**
Augustus	27 BC-AD 14
EARLY EMPIRE	**AD 14-192**
Julio-Claudian Dynasty	AD 14-68

Tiberius	14-37	Claudius	41-54
Caligula	37-41	Nero	54-68

Flavian Dynasty	69-96

Vespasian	69-79	Domitian	81-96
Titus	79-81		

Antonine Dynasty	96-192

Nerva	96-98	Antoninus Pius	138-161
Trajan	98-117	Marcus Aurelius	161-180
Hadrian	117-138	Commodus	180-192

LATER EMPIRE	**AD 192-395**
Severan Dynasty	193-235

Septimus Severus	193-211	Elagabalus	218-222
Caracalla	211-217	Severus Alexander	222-235

Military Anarchy	AD 235-284
Diocletian and the Tetrarchy	284-305
Dynasty of Constantine and Valentinian	AD 306-395

Constantine the Great	306-337	Valentinian and Valens	364-378
Sons of Constantine	337-361	Theodosius	379-395
Julian	361-363		

Division of the empire between Arcadius and Honorius	AD 395
Rome taken by Alaric	410
EASTERN EMPIRE	**after AD 395**

Theodosius II	408-450	Justinian	527-565

ARCHAIC GREEK ART

The first signs of art in the region of south-east Europe known today as Greece, go back to the Neolithic period, when the developing civilisation in the Near East came closer and closer to the Aegean world. The islands of the Cyclades, between Asia and Europe, were an essential link in the transmission of this culture. The third millennium BC, in fact, saw the emergence of a real civilisation at the heart of the Aegean. Although bronze metallurgy was spreading, the artists of these islands devoted themselves to giving shape to the marble won from their own soil. This is the reason for the existence of the large family of "Cycladic idols". They vary enormously in size and shape, being sometimes abstract and sometimes naturalistic, but always of harmonious proportions. Their purpose remains obscure; but their painted decoration, which has now disappeared, would probably have helped us to understand them.

In spite of this flowering of civilisation, the mainland world remained backward. Progressive and sometimes violent migrations of peoples from the Danubian area moved south to mix with natives of the Mediterranean area. These migrants were the ancestors of the Greeks, as has been proved by the decipherment of Linear B, their written script. At the end of the third millennium, however, another centre of civilisation rose in Crete, again because it was an island and was therefore spared from the troubles of the migrations. The Cretan language was written down in a hieroglyphic script and in the linear script known as Linear A; but all that is known of the language is that it was not Greek. Cretan civilisation came to a peak in an original form, in which the palace played an essential role. These palaces, at Knossos, Mallia and Phaistos, were once destroyed but were quickly rebuilt in an ambitious and remarkable style. They were not only political and social entities, but also artistic centres, which produced the refined creations of Minoan art, including their brilliant wall-painting.

The inventiveness and the freshness of Cretan decoration and objects have been brought to light by excavations in the island, and also by the excavations which Schliemann began at Mycenae. Indeed, in the famous grave-circle at Mycenae purely Minoan objects were associated with others, like the gold masks, which were cruder and different in spirit. This discovery shows the ambiguity of the Mycenaean civilisation. Mycenaean civilisation began in the 16th century BC and contributed to the destruction of the palaces of Crete about the middle of the millennium, and yet was also profoundly influenced by Crete's rich culture. Whether as imports or as prizes of war, the products of Minoan art are constantly found in Mycenaean ruins, either in their own right or in the pervasive influence of their naturalistic style. It was only gradually that Mycenaean creativity was to find an original artistic path, with a more rigorous and more abstract structure. After a number of setbacks Mycenaean civilisation in its turn disappeared in the serious general disorder throughout the Mediterranean Basin at the end of the 2nd millennium, when the Dorians, the last wave of Indo-European immigrants, arrived to complete the make-up of the Greek people.

After the silence of this destructive period, art was reborn under the discipline of geometry. Everything from vase decoration to pottery or bronze figurines was rigorously schematised, with every line subject to precise rules. But each region of Greece had its own application of this geometric law. In one place or another a motif or an ornament escaped the rule and showed a return to figurative art. In the decoration of Attic vases the human sil-

Head of woman
Fragment of a statue
Early Cycladic II
c 2700-2400 BC
Marble
Height 27 cm
Keros
Acquired in 1873
Rayet gift
MA 2709

13

houette was first rendered geometrically, but then imperceptibly took on an appearance closer to natural proportions. At the end of the 8th century BC "orientalising" art began, in which influences from the middle east became more frequent. These "oriental" motifs had been known for some time; but now they crowded into Greek art, only to be translated into expressions of Greek art, or rather into the various regional dialects which make up that single artistic language. The little Corinthian vases spread all over the Mediterranean Basin. In the middle of the 7th century BC, the period known now as "Protocorinthian", they achieved an extraordinary quality, which they were never to attain again. It was moreover in Corinth that the "black-figure" technique was devised for the decoration of vases with a black silhouette and with incised details. The technique was to spread quickly to all workshops. Those in Athens, however, and in the Cyclades, East Greece and Crete, amongst others, were undeveloped compared with this flowering of Corinthian artistic trade in the 7th century BC.

The decoration of such vases was exuberant; but sculpture at this time was austere. The 7th century is the age of the "Dedalic" style, which was a reaction against the fantasies of geometric art. It also saw the beginning of big sculpture in marble, which was produced both in the Cyclades and in Samos. The two major types of archaic statues now appeared, the *kouros*, a standing, athletic, naked young man, and the *kore*, a richly dressed young woman, also represented standing. This tradition was to go on to the end of the archaic period. The detail evolved; but the general theme, which was more conventional than for other types, such as the rider or the sphinx, was not changed. Each workshop put forward its own rendering of the human figure, and all in various ways evolved towards a common goal, a model closer to reality. The same development can be observed on the reliefs. They were particularly popular for gravestones, especially at Athens, and there are remarkable examples in architectural sculpture. On pediments, metopes and friezes sculptures of men eventually crowded out the monsters of primitive religion. There were more and more vases and small objects, put out by artistic centres which perpetuated the style of each city in figures and ornament but at the same time let other influences show through. The bronzes, for example, whether arms, statuettes, vessels or mirrors, testify to the rich sources inspiring the artist and to the predominance of certain popular styles in fashion.

Athenian pottery at first imitated Corinthian vessels, but then developed its own style, with original pictures which stressed the sense of the narrative. Athens was supreme in this form of expression, two of the finest artists being the Amasis Painter, a black-figure painter, and Exekias, a potter and painter who used the same technique. Corinthian vases ceased to compete with those of Athens, and those of Boeotia, Laconia and East Greece, good as they were, were also out-classed. Athens was also the place where the decisive change to "red-figure" pottery took place, about 530 BC. Instead of painting the figures black, the artist left them in the natural colour of the clay, silhouetted by the black background. With his brush he could then paint in on the figures a whole range of effects, far richer than those that could be produced on the black figures of the previous technique. The Andokides Painter was the pioneer of the new technique, though he did not exploit all its possibilities. It was Euphronios and his companions, at the end of the 6th century, who raised this technique to its peak. The silhouetted figures are full of movement, and their detailed anatomy seems to prepare the way for the fundamental change which was to overtake sculpture in the first quarter of the 5th century.

Spouted jug ("sauceboat")
Early Helladic, *c* 2500 BC
Gold — height 17 cm
Heraia, Arcadia (?)
Acquired in 1887
BJ 1885

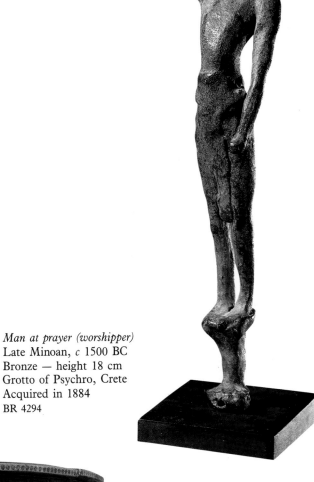

Man at prayer (worshipper)
Late Minoan, *c* 1500 BC
Bronze — height 18 cm
Grotto of Psychro, Crete
Acquired in 1884
BR 4294

Fragment of crater
Body laid out for burial (prothesis)
Attic — Late Geometric,
c 750 BC
Pottery — preserved height 58 cm
Dipylon Gate, Kerameikos,
Athens
Acquired in 1884
A 517

Pendant
Lion and eagle, with dropped janiform heads
Orientalising, Rhodian Dedalic, *c* 630 BC
Electrum — height 8.5 cm
Camirus, Rhodes
Département des Antiquités orientales
Salzmann Collection
BJ 2169

Loutrophoros (funerary vase)
Sphinxes, dances, and row of chariots
Protoattic, *c* 680 BC
Pottery — height 81 cm
Acquired in 1935
CA 2985

Funerary diadem
Lions, deer and ibex
Attic Geometric, *c* 750 BC
Gold — length 38.5 cm
Acquired in 1890
BJ 93

Fragment of griffin head
Cauldron attachment
Orientalising, 1st half of 7th century BC
Bronze — height preserved 10 cm
Acquired in 1864
BR 2614

Statuette decorating a tripod handle
Man with bull's head (Minotaur?)
Attic, late Geometric, *c* end of
8th century BC
Bronze — height 18 cm
Acquired in 1863 — Campana Collection
BR 104

Aryballos with head of woman
Combat and hare-hunt
Attributed to the Macmillan Painter
Protocorinthian, *c* 640 BC
Pottery — height 6.3 cm
Acquired in 1898
CA 931

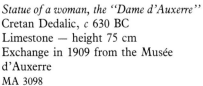

Statue of a woman, the "Dame d'Auxerre"
Cretan Dedalic, *c* 630 BC
Limestone — height 75 cm
Exchange in 1909 from the Musée
d'Auxerre
MA 3098

The "Lévy Oinochoe"
Fabulous animals and rows of wild goats
Orientalising, East Greek, *c* 650 BC
Pottery — height 39.5 cm
Acquired in 1891 — E. Lévy Collection
E 658

Dinos
Sphinxes and rows of animals
Orientalising, East Greek, *c* 615 BC
Pottery — height 35 cm
Cerveteri
Acquired in 1863 — Campana Collection
E 659

Column-crater
Herakles and Eurytion; row of horsemen
Early Corinthian, *c* 600 BC
Pottery — height 460 cm
Cerveteri
Campana Collection
E 635

Female head
Fragment of a statue of the Spédos
crossed-arms type
Early Cycladic II *c* 2700-2400 BC
Marble
Height 27 cm
Keros
Acquired in 1873 — Rayet gift
MA 2709

Torso of a Kouros
Naxian, *c* 560 BC
Marble — height 100 cm
Actium
Acquired in 1874
MA 687

Large-scale sculpture in marble was first made in the "Dedalic" style of the 7th century BC. In the following century it became more widespread, principally in the form of the two major types, the *kouros*, a nude young man, standing, his arms beside his body, his left leg forward, and the *kore*, a richly dressed young woman in the same position. Each regional centre, for example Naxos and Samos, put forward its own version of these common themes, in which permanent signs of a real style are to be found. But all the workshops converged in various ways towards an image which conformed more and more with reality.

Kore dedicated by Cheramyes
Samian, *c* 570 BC
Marble — height 192 cm
Sanctuary of Hera, Samos
Acquired in 1881
MA 686

Tripod pyxis
Birth of Athena,
attributed to Painter C
Attic black-figured, *c* 570 BC
Pottery — height 14 cm
Acquired in 1894
CA 616

Mirror handle
Woman standing, carrying a crown
Corinthian, *c* 600-590 BC
Bronze — height 38.4 cm
Acquired in 1889
BR 1684

Tripod support
Kneeling Gorgon
1st half of 6th century BC
Bronze — height 55 cm
In the sea off Rhodes
Acquired in 1883
BR 2570

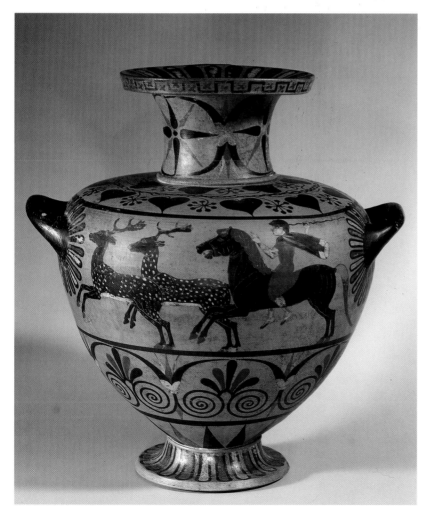

Cup (skyphos)
Seduction scenes, courtship presents
Attributed to the Amasis Painter
Attic black-figured, *c* 550 BC
Pottery — height 11,5 cm
Camirus, 1860, Salzmann excavations
Acquired in 1879 — Parent Collection
A 479

Hydria
Hunting scene
Black-figured Etrusco-Ionian,
c 540-530 BC
Pottery — height 40.5 cm
Cerveteri
Acquired in 1863 — Campana Collection
E 697

Head of the "Rampin horseman"
The head fits the torso of a horseman in
the Acropolis Museum, which is one of a
group of two horsemen : Hippias and
Hipparchus ? Castor and Pollux ?
Attic, *c* 550-540 BC
Marble — height 27 cm (head)
Acquired in 1846
G. Rampin bequest
MA 3104

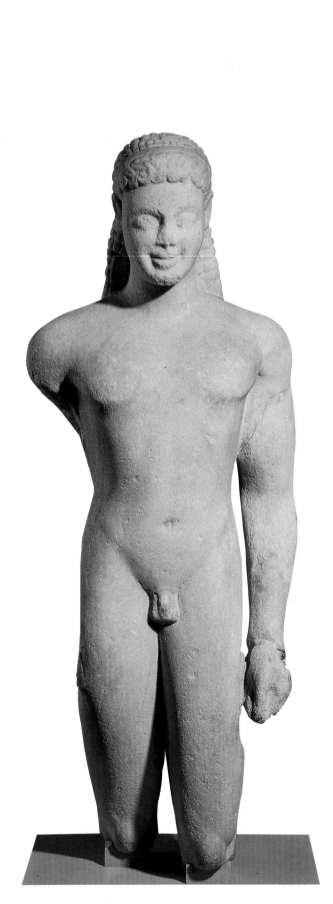

Kouros
Parian, *c* 540 BC
Marble — height 105 cm
Paros, near the sanctuary of Asklepios
Acquired in 1910
MA 3101

Reliefs from the Temple of Athena at Assos (Mysia)
Two metopes : centaur, boar. Block from frieze : Herakles feasting
c 540-520 BC

Andesite — height 77 cm (metopes), 81 cm (frieze)
Acquired in 1838 — Gift of Sultan Mahmoud II
MA 2826, MA 2827, MA 2829

Amphora and cover
Herakles' fight with the three-bodied monster, Geryon
Signed by the potter Exekias, attributed to Group E
Attic black-figured,
c 540 BC
Pottery — height 50 cm (with the cover)
Acquired in 1883
F 53

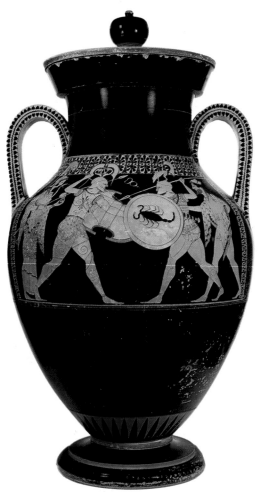

The potters at Athens revolutionized the art of painted pottery. They reversed the relationship which was established by the black-figure style, in which the painted motif, with incised details, stood out darkly on a bright background colour, which was left untouched. From now on, however, on red-figure pottery, the background was filled in with dark colour, leaving the figures in the bright background colour silhouetted, a rich series of details being added with a brush. In a single generation the red-figure potters dominated the new technique, as the work of Euphronios shows. This was the end of the Archaic period, and the human figure became supreme in the potters' work, as in the other arts and the other creative disciplines.

Amphora
Fight between two warriors in the presence
of Athena and Hermes
Signed by the potter Andokides, attributed
to the Andokides Painter
Attic red-figured, *c* 530 BC
Pottery — height 58 cm
Vulci
Acquired in 1843 — Prince de Canino
Collection
G 1

Chalice-crater
Wrestling-match between Herakles
and the giant Antaios
Signed by the painter Euphronios
Attic red-figured, *c* 510 BC
Pottery — height 46 cm
Cerveteri
Acquired in 1863 — Campana Collection
G 103

Fragment of acroterion
Head of sphinx
Corinthian, *c* 530 BC
Pottery — height 18 cm
Thebes
Acquired in 1895
CA 637

Mirror support
Young woman (kore) standing on a stool
Aeginetan (?), 1st quarter
of 5th century BC
Bronze — height 18 cm
Acquired in 1888
BR 1688

Statuette of a butcher
The butcher is braining a piglet on the block
Boeotian, beginning of 5th century BC
Pottery — height 12 cm
Thebes
Acquired in 1902
CA 1455

Cup
Theseus and Amphitrite, in the presence
of Athena
Signed by the potter Euphronios,
attributed to the painter Onesimos
Attic red-figured, *c* 500-490 BC
Pottery — height 16.5 cm,
diameter 40 cm
Cerveteri
Acquired in 1871
G 104

Cup
Eos carrying the corpse of her son Memnon
Signed by the potter Kaliades and the
painter Douris
Attic red-figured, *c* 490 BC
Pottery — height 12 cm, diameter 26.8 cm
Santa Maria di Capua
Acquired in 1879 — Prince Napoleon
Collection
G 115

Cup
Phoenix and Achilles' captive, Briseis
Signed by the potter Brygos,
attributed to the Brygos painter
Attic red-figured, *c* 490 BC
Pottery — height 13.4 cm,
diameter 32.5 cm
Italy
Acquired in 1881
Bammeville Collection
G 152

The beginning of the 5th century BC was a troubled period in the political history of Greece, when it was threatened by the Persian invasions. It was nevertheless the age of gold and of Attic pottery, and even veiled allusions to the political events are scarcely to be found in art. Images including historical personalities, like Croesus on the *amphora by Myson*, are quite exceptional. It is much more usual for masters like Onesimos, Douris or the Brygos painter, to find their inspiration in mythology, and they normally respected the shape of the vessel to be respected, all being very clever at finding a way round the restrictions of placing of decoration within a medallion.

Amphora
Croesus on his funeral-pyre, to which
his servant Euthymos is setting light
Attributed to the painter Myson
Attic red-figured, *c* 500-490 BC
Pottery — height 59 cm
Vulci *c* 1829
Acquired in 1836 — Durand Collection
G 197

CLASSICAL GREEK ART

The transition from the 6th to the 5th century BC was a troubled period for the Greek world. In the east the Greek cities of Ionia were trying to shake off Persian domination, and there was the danger of invasion. A conflict followed, in which Greece was twice to be invaded by armies, the first belonging to Darius, and the second, ten years later, to Xerxes. Marathon, Salamis and Plataea were hallowed, historic victories for the triumphant cities, Athens above all; but they are also key dates in the history of Greek civilisation, in particular for its art. This period was the turning-point, when statues in the new, easy pose appear almost everywhere on Greek soil. Transitional works like the *torso from Miletus* combine a certain stiffness and over-emphasis of the anatomy, which survive from Archaic art, with a sense of real balance, natural asymmetry and free movement introduced by the dawn of Classicism. In the Severe style, which began at this time, faces were both more serious and more expressive of the inner life. The athlete replaced the *kouros*, and in the situations that they were portraying the artists were often looking for the moment which showed the greatest psychological effect, rather than the moment when an action had taken place. Examples are one of the sides of the calyx krater in the Louvre which is attributed to the Niobid Painter, and the east pediment of the Temple of Zeus at Olympia. The fragments of the metopes of the temple of Zeus, also in the Louvre, show how art had developed since the beginning of the 5th century BC. In the Peloponnese, Athens, Ionia and the western Greek colonies, the creation of statues of athletes, often in bronze, produced powerful forms with realistic postures and convincing movements. Many of these were made, but only a few such big bronzes have come down to us. Nevertheless the figurines, which are in a great variety of attitudes and styles, demonstrate the importance of the movement which produced the *Diskobolos of Myron*.

Pottery continued to be decorated in the red-figure technique, but side by side with it, in the middle of the 5th century BC, the "white-ground" technique, which had been known since the Archaic period, became more popular. At first this decoration was fixed by firing, normally using only two colours. From about the middle of the 5th century BC, however, a less durable technique was used, in which, after a whitish clay base had been fired on, a wash of more lively though fugitive colours was applied. These delicate works of art, such as lekythoi, are to be found particularly among offerings to the dead, in other words among objects which would receive scarcely any handling.

After the end of the Persian Wars Athens played the leading role in the history of Greece. In the third quarter of the 5th century BC the Delian Confederacy and the government of Pericles were to reinforce this supremacy. This was the peak of Classical civilisation, marked by the great works undertaken on the Athenian Acropolis. The building of the Parthenon and the creation of its sculptured decoration were to have a profound effect on the evolution of art. The metopes, the frieze and the pediments not only bear witness to the diverse styles and talents of those involved, but also they express above all the unity of Pheidias' inspired programme. The *metope from the Parthenon* now in the Louvre shows that the Severe style had not entirely disappeared about 440 BC; but the metope was inspired by the same spirit as that which was responsible for creating the Ergastines (or Arrephoroi — the girls carrying the peplos) on the Parthenon frieze.

Calyx krater Apollo and Artemis kill the daughters of Niobe and are guilty of sacrilegious pride Attributed to the Niobid Painter (The name comes from this vase) Attic red-figured. c 460 BC Pottery Height 54 cm Near Orvieto in 1880 Acquired in 1883 Tyskiewicz Collection G 341

31

Both groups are a triumph of the human form, a celebration of the virtues of proportion and balance, and a happy marriage of the ideal and the real. The same values can be observed in the free-standing sculpture, particularly in the types created by the bronze-master Polyclitus, an artist from the Peloponnese, who had come to exercise his talents at Athens. Balance is the most obvious element in his powerful statues of athletes; but it is a shifting balance which links rest and movement. The slope of the hips is matched by the opposite slope of the shoulders. The limp arm at rest slips backwards, while the heel of the taut leg is raised. As a result a dynamic is created in the structure of a statue like the *Doryphoros* or the *Diadoumenos* by the alternating response of the different parts of the body in relation to a median axis across it. Polyclitus and the other great masters of this generation, such as Pheidias, Agorakritos, Alcamenes and Kresilas, must have had the feeling of having achieved the end of a long evolution which had begun with earliest Archaism.

The Peloponnesian War soaked the last third of the 5th century BC in blood. The established order was to be upset, in particular the artistic order of things. At Athens, by the end of the century, the return to Ionic architecture, the discreet appearance of melancholy on faces, the accentuation of hips on bodies to the point of imbalance, the taste for clinging "dampfold" drapery, all show that the idealism of high Classicism had already passed. Scenes on vases show the same tendencies, while they begin to show themes rarely used before, such as the life of women or pictures of childhood. The manufacture of painted vases, moreover, declined very markedly at the turning-point between the 5th and 4th centuries BC. Vase-painting only sprang to life again about 370 BC with the "Kertch" style, so-called because its products were largely exported to barbarian kingdoms of the Crimean peninsula and southern Russia. At the same time as this last period of good Attic pottery, the Greeks in the west were in full production of "Italiot" vases, which came from the south Italian workshops in Lucania, Apulia and Campania. This varied 4th-century flowering of several regional styles began with the emigration of Athenian potters to Magna Graecia, southern Italy. The decoration of these pots reflected not only the influence of the theatre and of large-scale painting, but also the numerous facets of a world in which Greek colonists mixed with Italic peoples.

Sculpture passed through a phase of realism in reaction to the idealism of high Classicism. There then came some great artists, whose style was to have influence far beyond the boundaries of Classicism. Praxiteles regarded with distaste the powerful bodies of athletic heroes, preferring the ambiguous charms of sinuous young men, and the grace of the female body. He was the first to show the female body nude, when he made the famous *Aphrodite of Knidos*. While Praxiteles' sculptures were full of dreamy melancholy, Scopas' works were imbued with boiling passion. He loved to torment their bodies and to wrack their faces. Some slabs from the frieze of the Mausoleum at Halicarnassus carry his fiery mark. The imbalance of many of his subjects shows the way things had gone since the middle of the 5th century BC. Shapes kept their Classical envelope; but the content had changed and was impregnated with new values. Artists were inspired by quite different things. They were preoccupied now with attention to the individual, the expression of emotion, and curiosity about the barbarian world. Fundamentally the subsequent Hellenistic period was only to develop tendencies which had already appeared in the course of the 4th century BC, though Alexander's adventure was to give it a definitive stamp.

A monument like the *relief from the Passage of the Theores* demonstrates very well the transition between Archaic forms and the first images of Classicism. The three Graces, in a panel, have kept the attitude and the dress of *korai*. Hermes' gesture is a bold way of opening up the space in front of him, and it symbolizes the freedom of these silhouetted figures in comparison with the stiffness that had constrained them for more than a century. The bronze statuette from Phocis also gives a feeling that the sculpting of a body at ease, close to reality, is not far away. From now on, the mobile figure of the athlete was to replace the rigidity of the *kouros*.

Male Statuette
Man in the attitude of a suppliant
Sicyonian. *c* 480 BC
Bronze — height 26.4 cm
Phocis
Acquired in 1937 — David-Weill gift
BR 4236

Reliefs from the Passage of the Theores
Hermes and the Graces
Thasian, *c* 470 BC
Marble - height 92 cm
Thasos in 1864 (Miller Mission)
Acquired in 1864 — given by the
Emperor Napoleon III
MA 696

Helmeted female head
Athena
Aeginetan, *c* 460 BC
Marble — height 28 cm
Acquired in 1917 — Vogüé gift
MA 3109

The *Torso of Miletus* shows how the previous artificial equilibrium in sculptured bodies was replaced by a realistic balance. The same change can be seen on faces, on which conventional smiles were replaced by serious expressions. This led on to features which were even more severe, with deeply shaped eyes which revealed inner feelings. It was not only action which was now of interest, but also the intentions which preceded action or thoughts in the course of action. The *Athena of Aegina* or the *Heracles of Olympia* for example, are not simply representations of a god and a hero, while the *Stele of Pharsalos* is bathed in mystery and gentle melancholy because of the looks exchanged by the figures. From now on the face is the mirror of the soul.

Male torso
Ionian (by Pythagoras?), after 479 BC
Marble — height 132 cm
Ruins of the theatre at Miletus
(Rayet-Thomas excavations)
Acquired in 1873 — Rothschild gift
MA 2792

Fragment of a metope from the temple of Zeus
Head of Herakles (Herakles
and the Kerynitian stag)
c 460 BC
Marble — height 32.5 cm
Olympia (Morea scientific expedition)
Acquired in 1829
Gift of the Greek Assembly
MA 724 (a)

Gravestone, "Glorifying of
the flower"
Two girls face to face,
carrying flowers
and purses of seed (?)
Thessalian, *c* 460 BC
Marble — height 60 cm
Acquired in 1862
Leon Heuzey mission
MA 701

Statuette of Herakles
The hero is brandishing his club
Argive, *c* 460-4500 BC
Bronze — height 13 cm
Mantinea
Acquired in 1923
BR 4171

Statuette of male wearing boots
Dionysos
Argive, *c* 460-4500 BC
Bronze — height 22.5 cm
Olympia
Acquired in 1894
BR 154

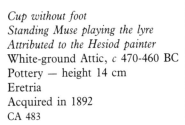

Cup without foot
Standing Muse playing the lyre
Attributed to the Hesiod painter
White-ground Attic, *c* 470-460 BC
Pottery — height 14 cm
Eretria
Acquired in 1892
CA 483

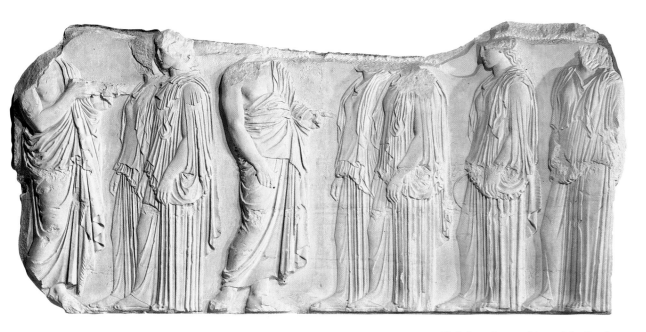

Slab from the east frieze of the Parthenon
Great Panathenaic procession :
organizers and ergastines (peplos-bearers)
c 440 BC
Marble — height 96 cm
Athens Acropolis
Seized in the Revolution
Choiseul-Gouffier Collection
MA 738

Metope no. 11 from the south
frieze of the Parthenon
Centaur and female Lapith
447-440 BC
Marble — height 135 cm
Athens Acropolis
Acquired in 1818
Choiseul-Gouffier Collection
MA 736

Male torso
Copy of a bronze statue of Polyclitus,
the ''Diadumenos'', made c 440 BC
Roman period
Marble — height 111 cm
Acquired in 1863 — Campana Collection
MA 1027

C lassical art's aspiration to the ideal developed from the Severe Style of the early classical period. This development, however, was in no way inevitable, and the idealization of artistic forms only came about through the creation of the art of the Parthenon. Forms free of space and time were imbued with balance and harmony, with clarity and reason, and with calm and serenity. Polyclitus' athletes are like this. The faultless musculature of their bodies encloses a spirit that can never be touched by the irrational. But this special moment lasted only a short time, no more than a generation. The Peloponnesian War and its horrors shook all certainties and changed the spirit of art. The aryballos-like little lekythos, for example, evokes a woman's world that not long ago took second place to masculine values, while the bronze athlete with its realistic stance has now become part of the human world.

Gravestone
The inscription shows that the deceased
was Sosinos, from Gortyna, a bronze-
founder : the double shape under his chair
represents the bellows for his forge.
Attic, last quarter of 5th century BC
Marble — height 100 cm
Piraeus
Acquired in 1817 — Fauvel Collection
MA 769

Statuette of a man
Boxer
First quarter of 4th century BC
Bronze — height 20 cm
Acquired in 1939 — Rayet gift
BR 4240

Aryballic lekythos
Scene of women
Attributed to the Meidias Painter
Attic red-figured, *c* 4500 BC
Pottery
Acquired in 1889
CA 254

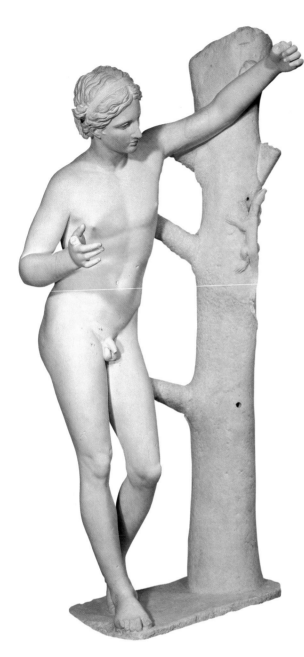

Apollo Sauroctonos (the lizard-killer)
Copy of an original attributed to
Praxiteles and made c 350 BC
Roman
Marble — height 149 cm
Acquired in 1808 — Borghese Collection
MA 441

Gravestone of Phainippos and Mnesarete
Family reunion and hand-shake
Attic, *c* 350 BC
Marble — height 148 cm
Attica
Acquired in 1879
MA 767

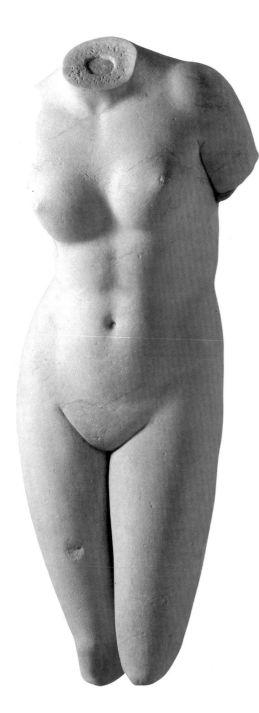

The Hellenism of the fourth century BC kept the appearance of Classicism; but at the same time it was shot through with a crisis which affected equally creativity and society and the economy. A new sensibility was born, which encouraged the expression of individual values which had previously been subordinated to the ideals of the state. The latter were no longer enough, and the expressions of religion changed, too. Sorrow was no longer forbidden on gravestones, even though its expression was still muted. Pain was shown more strongly on the faces of the suitors struck by Odysseus' arrows. The *Apollo* of Praxiteles shows an ambiguous adolescent, no longer the mighty god or previously redoubtable archer. And the Athenian master-artist pays particular tribute to the sensual female body, which he shows nude for the first time.

Bell-crater
Massacre of the suitors by Odysseus
and Telemachus
Attributed to the Ixion Painter
Campanian, *c* 330 BC
Pottery — height 40 cm
Acquired in 1985
CA 5724

Aphrodite
Aphrodite of Cnidus type
Copy of an original in marble, attributed
to Praxiteles and made c 350 BC
Roman
Marble — height 122 cm
Formerly in the Luxembourg Gardens
MA 2184

*Head of Aphrodite, the Kauffmann Head
Copy of the Aphrodite of Cnidus by
Praxiteles, made in the 2nd century BC*
Marble — height 35 cm
Acquired in 1951
Von Kauffmann Collection
MA 3518

The fourth century BC explored the female image eagerly. The following century reinforced this tendency at all levels of art. Whether in the Tanagra figurines, so elegant with their smart hair and made cheerful with bright colours, or in the opulent nudity of large-scale statues, artists never ceased to be stimulated and inspired by the female body. The number of representations of Aphrodite grew and grew, with variations in attitude, height and material. The stamp of the leading artists of the later classical period on this repertoire was permanent, as is shown by the long-lasting fashion for a type like the *Aphrodite of Cnidus*. As for the *crouching Aphrodite*, the theme has never ceased to haunt artists' imaginations, and reflections of it can even be seen in contemporary art.

Female statuette
Boeotian, Tanagra, *c* 320 BC
Pottery — height 32 cm
Acquired in 1874
MNB 585

From the Archaic period on, winged figures occur frequently in Greek art. Love, for example, is introduced into the repertoire of images in the form of a young man equipped with wings. In the Hellenistic centuries he was made younger and younger, until he looked like a chubby little child, whose games were often cruel and whose mischievousness was punished from time to time by his mother Aphrodite. The idea of victory (*Nike*) was also given shape very early as a winged young woman. As a result she was naturally swift-moving, she could not be foreseen, and her nature was divine. Victories appear as a symbol of success in every generation and in every style. They are found on the one hand at Myrina, where their airy crowd flit over the walls of the tombs, on the other hand at Samothrace, where the most majestic of all Victories beat the air with her powerful wings.

Medallion
Bust of Eros
3rd century BC
Gold and garnets
Diameter 9.42 cm
De Clerq-Boisgelin gift
BJ 2248

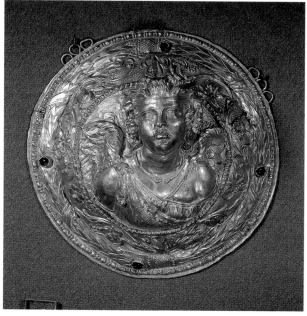

Statuette of Victory
Attributed to the Victories Coroplast
c beginning of 2nd century BC
Terracotta — height 27.8 cm
Excavations at Myrina
Deposited by the Museum of the
University of Lyon in 1963
LY 1651

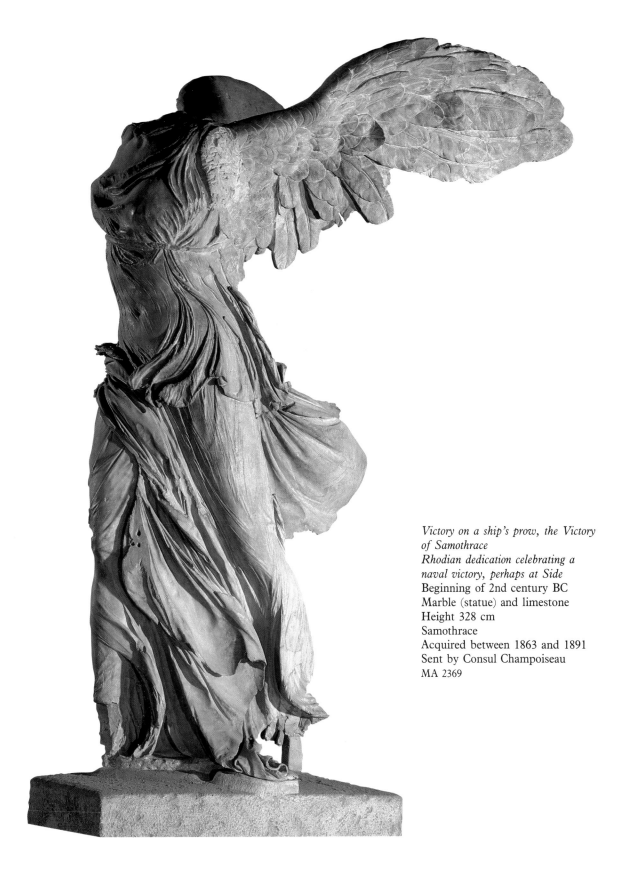

*Victory on a ship's prow, the Victory
of Samothrace
Rhodian dedication celebrating a
naval victory, perhaps at Side*
Beginning of 2nd century BC
Marble (statue) and limestone
Height 328 cm
Samothrace
Acquired between 1863 and 1891
Sent by Consul Champoiseau
MA 2369

Statuette of a bearded man fighting
Pergamene, middle of 2nd century BC
Bronze with incrusted silver and red
copper — height 25 cm
Acquired in 1950 — Jameson Collection
BR 4307

Statuette of a negro
Chained slave
2nd century BC
Bronze — height 13 cm
The Fayum
Acquired in 1892
BR 361

In the immense world defined by the conquests of Alexander, the sculptors of the Hellenistic period explored subjects which were unacceptable in Classical art. Instead of the impassive faces of the fifth century, which were symbols of order and harmony, the new artists produced in contrast the anguished face of the Silenus waiting for his punishment, or the poignant expression of the old Centaur tortured by love. A taste for exoticism exchanged the balanced athletes of the previous period for the dislocated outline of the young black man. And yet the emphasized pathos of the thoroughly Pergamene Jameson statuette retained every aspect of the Classical theme of gods with raised arm doing battle.

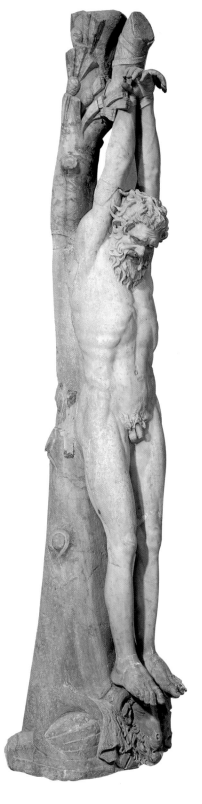

Centaur ridden by Eros
Copy of an original of 2nd century BC
Roman
Marble — height 147 cm
Rome in 17th century
Acquired in 1808 — Borghese Collection
MA 562

Anguish of Marsyas
Marsyas, hung from a tree on the orders
of Apollo, whom he had offended,
was condemned to be flayed alive by
a Scythian slave
Copy, after a Pergamene model
of the end of the 3rd century BC
Roman
Marble — height 256 cm
Acquired in 1808 — Borghese Collection
MA 542

Sleeping hermaphrodite
The mattress is an addition by Bernini
Copy after an original of the 2nd century BC
Roman
Marble — length 148 cm
Rome in 16th century
Acquired in 1808 — Borghese Collection
MA 231

Warrior,
the "Borghese Gladiator"
c 50 BC
Marble — height 199 cm
Nettuno at beginning
of 17th century
Acquired in 1808
Borghese Collection
MA 527

The final period of Greek sculpture was marked by a clear return to the artistic principles of the fifth and fourth centuries BC. This revival of the themes of the past was encouraged by the haunting presence of the memorials of a glorious past, but also by the admiration of the invading Romans, conquered by Classicism, who ordered copies. The *Gladiator of Agasias* recalls the Severe style, the *Venus de Milo* recalls works by Phidias and Praxiteles, and the perfect body of the *Hermaphrodite* can be included in the list of figures that cannot be improved on. At the same time, however, its bizarre nature and the ambiguity of its pose, the restless anatomy of the *Venus*, and the *Gladiator*'s display of musculature make them of their time, which was a twilight period, though a superb twilight.

Aphrodite, the "Venus de Milo"
The right arm was in front,
with the hand at the level of the left
thigh. The left arm was raised.
Classicizing, *c* 100 BC
Marble — height 204 cm
Melos in 1820
Acquired in 1821
MA 399

ETRUSCAN ART

In pre-Roman Italy Etruscan civilisation stands out as the most brilliant. Even if there is still some mystery as to its beginnings, there is general agreement that it was not the result of the arrival of a foreign people, but rather an evolution in the way of life of populations already there. At the beginning of the 10th century BC, a culture came into being which is now named after Villanova, a site near Bologna where a key feature was the increasing use of iron. The discovery of its cemeteries has brought to light its funerary customs. Biconical urns of coarse pottery placed in pits contained the remains of the deceased, flanked by ceremonial objects or by objects from daily life, such as brooches, bracelets and razors which accompanied the dead man in his life beyond the tomb. There were sometimes even more ambitious objects, such as the *bronze throne* in the Louvre. All these objects were decorated with geometric motifs, which occasionally included very schematised silhouettes of animals or men. The sheet or cast bronze was worked in repoussé or engraved. The hand-made pottery, constructed without a wheel, was covered with incised details. The decorative repertoire shows that there were contacts not only with the Mediterranean civilisations, but also with the Halstatt culture. It was when the first Greeks arrived that the period came to an end, marked by profound changes — the appearance of the potter's wheel, of refined clay and of painted pottery, and the introduction of the first "orientalizing" motifs, together with the first Phoenician and Egyptian imports.

This orientalization is a characteristic of Etruscan art between the middle of the 8th century BC and the beginning of the 6th century BC, and it is part of the real birth of Etruscan civilisation. The first explorers who sailed in from the east were attracted by the metal-bearing ores of the area. The development of trade made certain towns rich, particularly in the south, and promoted the growth of an aristocratic class. Trade with the Middle East and Greece brought to Etruscan territory foreign artists. The Etruscans were very receptive to their influences and quickly showed their ability in the field of goldwork. The jewellery found in the princely tombs of Cerveteri and Praeneste shows what their craftsmen were capable of. At the opposite end of the scale from gold, the Etruscan potters used the more modest medium of clay for products which closely imitated models from Corinth. "Bucchero" pottery, on the other hand, was their own invention. This pottery was made of fairly fine clay, was entirely black, and was often decorated in relief or with incised motifs. It appeared in the second quarter of the 7th century BC in shapes which imitated metal. There was prolific production of this pottery, which was centred principally at Cerveteri, and which was to stay in fashion until the 5th century BC. Its sculptured shapes of various sizes were part of the general orientalising movement. But quite quickly the influences from the east were to pass through the filter of Greek creativity, which was to fascinate Etruscan artists so much that their work became part of its own history.

From the second quarter of the 6th century BC, the signs of this Greek influence are easily discerned. Peloponnesian style prevailed at first, for example in the powerful "Dedalic" sculptures produced in volcanic stone, though without an understanding of the style's organic coherence. Then the spirit of Ionian art was spread wider and wider by artists from the Greek cities in Asia Minor. It influenced most disciplines, and wall-painting in particular sprang into life in a marvellous way. The world recreated on the

Oinochoe in the shape of the head of a young man c 425-400 BC Bronze Height 30 cm Gabii Malmaison Collection BR 2955

walls of the tombs, above all in Tarquinia, shows both Greek influence and also the wish to surround the deceased with images of real life. The cemeteries and sanctuaries of the Etruscans have also yielded Attic vases, which the Etruscans imported en masse. The Greek myths seem not always to have been understood, and the Attic style was in the end to be replaced by Ionicizing tendencies. Side by side with this mixed art the "Canopic jars" of Chiusi continued in a spirit which was without foreign influences and which followed ancient funerary customs. Pottery, furthermore, was a material of choice. Pottery ornaments were used to cover the superstructure of temples, whether the most modest antefix or the acroteria from Portonaccio statues whose creation cannot be explained simply in terms of foreign influence. The *Campana plaques* were also made of pottery. The painted scenes which covered these facing plaques from buildings are not understood; but they are done with extraordinary decorative skill. Finally, pottery was used for the *Sarcophagus of a Man and Wife* from Cerveteri, a remarkable masterpiece of the end of the 6th century BC. This is one of the most attractive products of Etruscan art. Etruscan art also excelled in the manufacture of bronzes, a natural development because of the abundance of the raw material. Numerous workshops, particularly at Vulci, produced vessels, candelabra and incense-burners. They were enlivened by figurines with an intense sense of movement, even though the anatomical structure is not always well rendered.

All these shapes matched perfectly the spirit of Archaic art, in which decorative values and lively attitudes commanded attention. Although the transition to the Classical style inspired Greek art, this is not the case for Etruscan art. The first evidence of decline had appeared in the country, and their artists did not succeed in keeping up with the evolution which came to fruition, for example, in Greek sculpture. They seem to have been late in taking note of the changes. Although a few Etruscan works of this period were successes, the abstractness and the eternal balance of Classicism was never realised in their work. Moreover, the sources of Greek influence declined. Many Attic vases still arrived in Etruria in the first half of the century; but in the second half of the century the number can be seen to have declined. At the end of the 5th century BC, however, there was a noticeable revival in contacts with the Greek world, especially from southern Italy. A great deal of bronze-working continued, as is shown by the panoplies of armour and the engraved mirrors from the 4th century BC. At this time the local pottery also had to face a demand which was no longer satisfied by imports. This was the reason why Etruscan red-figured pottery sprang into being, often displacing adaptations and imitations of earlier periods. Wall-painting continued to develop, and individualized faces appeared. At the end of the 4th century BC buildings began to be constructed on which terracotta architectural decoration was imbued with the style of Praxiteles, though it was not popular with following generations. At this period, when the Romans were expanding and were gradually annexing Etruscan territory, there was a marked revival of Greek influence, particularly the "Pergamene" style, which has left its traces on the last Etruscan products. The multi-faceted Greek art of the portrait had an influence on the numerous votive heads created at this time. In addition, the decoration of the usually mediocre big terracotta sarcophagi made in Etruria in the 2nd century BC, of the terracotta cinerary urns from Chiusi, and of the alabaster cinerary urns from Volterra combined Hellenistic pathos with the harshest realism. The modelling of the fine bronze male *head from Fiesole* is so sensitive and immediate that it can be considered one of the last works of art that can truly be called Etruscan, made by a people who were finally absorbed into the Roman world.

Helmet
Villanovan, 2nd half of 8th century BC
Bronze — height 40 cm
Acquired in 1967
BR 4399

V illanovan art was a prologue to Etruscan art. Its qualities are amply demonstrated in the pottery, and even more happily in the bronze objects. The repoussé motifs on the metal are like geometric figures. The helmet was used as a lid for a biconical cinerary urn. It was derived from an Urnfield prototype, and it was made of two sheets of metal riveted together, decorated with circles, bosses and little raised dots. Its presence may indicate that the tomb belonged to a warrior, and it certainly demonstrates the existence of an aristocratic class. The decoration of the throne more ambitiously introduces human and animal figures, integrated with the geometric motifs. This object demonstrates that there was belief in an after-life as early as the first half of the seventh century BC.

Funerary throne
Villanovan, first half of 7th century BC
Bronze — height 460 cm
Acquired in 1967
BR 4406

Krater and support
Orientalising, second half
of 7th century BC
Coarse pottery (impasto)
Height 132 cm
Acquired in 1863
Campana Collection
CP 2682

Brooch
Heads of deer. Etruscan inscription
in granulation on the bow
c 630 BC
Gold — length 216 cm
Chiusi
BJ 816

Tripod vase
The handle is sculpted
in the shape of an animal
Villanovan, second half
of 7th century BC
Coarse pottery (impasto)
Height 17.5 cm
Acquired in 1954
CA 3450

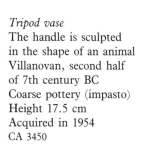

Pendant
Head of the river-god Achelous
Beginning of 5th century BC
Gold — height 4 cm
Acquired in 1863
Campana Collection
BJ 498

Canopic jar
The arms are moveable
Second half of 6th century BC
Terracotta — height 50 cm
Chiusi
Acquired in 1851
D 162

Vessel in form of a leg
A face is sculpted on the front
Second half of 6th century BC
Pottery (bucchero) — height 24 cm
Acquired in 1863 — Campana Collection
C 719

The Etruscans' vivid sense of religion gave the sacred a leading role in their works of art. The antefix with a female head has a smiling grace which comes from Ionia but which was tempered by Attic influence. It evokes the rich decoration of the temples. Architectural terracottas gave both practical and magical protection to many points of the structure. The other three objects are all funerary art. The plaque of a cippus from Chiusi shows the laying-out of a corpse in an Etruscan ritual. The mysterious scenes on the revetment plaques from Cerveteri tell us something of the luxuriousness of certain tombs. In particular, the *Sarcophagus of a man and wife*, which is a masterpiece of Etruscan art, gives us a surprising image for antiquity by showing a couple in which the woman is the equal of the man.

Antefix with female face
Beginning of 5th century BC
Pottery — height 26 cm
Cerveteri
Acquired in 1863 — Campana Collection
CP 5164

The Man and Wife Sarcophagus
End of 6th century BC
Pottery — height 114 cm
Cerveteri
Acquired in 1863 — Campana
Collection
CP 5194

Funerary relief
Laying-out of a corpse and funerary rites
c 490-480 BC
Stone — height 38 cm
MA 3602

Architectural revetment plaques
Two old men seated, sacrifice scene (?)
End of 6th century BC
Pottery — height 123 cm
Cerveteri
Acquired in 1863 — Campana Collection
CP 6626 and 6628

Engraved mirror
Oeneus, Atalanta, Meleager and Peleus
End of 4th century BC
Bronze — height 21.4 cm
Acquired in 1825 — Durand Collection
BR 1749

Candelabrum
Dancer with rattles
Beginning of 5th century BC

Bronze
Height 43 cm
BR 3145

Stamnos
Dionysiac scene
Etruscan red-figured, end of
4th century BC
Pottery — height 35 cm
Vulci
Acquired in 1977
Fould Collection
CA 6530

Vase in form of a duck (askos)
Winged female genius
Chiusi group, second half of 4th
century BC
Pottery — height 11.5 cm
Acquired in 1863 — Campana Collection
H 100

Elongated female statuette
Aphrodite ?
c 350 BC
Bronze — height 50.5 cm
Acquired in 1898
Tyskiewicz Collection
BR 321

Cover of a cinerary urn
Elderly man holding a garland and a phiale
Second half of 2nd century BC
Pottery — height 35 cm
Chiusi
S 868

During the Hellenistic period Etruscan civilization was in decline, and their cities were being weakened by the struggle with Rome. Many works at this time lack inspiration. And yet vivacity, emotion and the sense of reality found in Hellenistic art were perfectly in accord with the Etruscan spirit. Indeed, although mediocre craftsmen produced dull versions of the Pergamene style, the master who sculpted the cover of a cinerary urn from Chiusi knew how to enliven the dead man's profile, and how to give the feeling of a familiar expression. In another group, on the alabaster urn from Volterra, we are presented, under the clumsy effigy of the deceased, with an interesting relief which relates belief about death and daily life, showing a Gallic cart carrying the dead man to the life beyond. As for the head from Fiesole, it is close to being a portrait such as Rome was to cultivate with great enthusiasm.

Cinerary Urn
Woman with fan; journey by cart
to the other world
c 100 BC
Alabaster — height 84 cm
Volterra
Acquired in 1827 — Micali Collection
MA 2357

Juba I
Portrait of the King of Numidia, an ally
of Pompey
End of 1st century BC
Marble — height 45 cm
Cherchel
Acquired in 1895
MA 1885

R oman art at the beginning often echoed the different currents of Greek art, sometimes juxtaposing
them in eclectic works. The *relief of Domitius Ahenobarbus* is an example, in which a Greek repertoire and Greek
expression are used side by side with features of local
life. The effigy of an unknown venerable senator is shown
emotively, and the sense of reality helps to give a permanent sense of character. This can easily be fitted into
the development of the Hellenistic portrait, while the
idealized majesty of the *head of the Numidian King Juba I*
could easily pass for that of a god from Classical Greece.

Portrait of a senator
Sometimes identified as Aulus Postumius
Albinus
c 100 BC
Marble — height 37.5 cm
Acquired in 1888
MA 919

Cup with concave sides (modiolus)
Skeletons at a feast, in the spirit of Epicurus
Boscoreale Treasure, 1st century AD
Silver, partly gilded — height 10.4 cm
Boscoreale, near Pompeii
Acquired in 1895 — Rothschild gift
BJ 1923

Winged genius
Decoration from the peristyle of the villa
of Publius Fannius Sinistor
3rd quarter of 1st century AD
Wall-painting — height 126 cm
Boscoreale, near Pompeii
Acquired in 1903
P 23

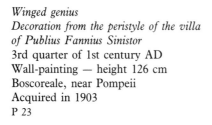

Emblema bowl
Allegory of Alexandria?
Boscoreale Treasure, end of 1st
century AD
Gilded silver — diameter 22.5 cm
Boscoreale, near Pompeii
Acquired in 1895 — Rothschild gift
BJ 1969

"Domitius Ahenobarbus" relief
Census and sacrifice to Mars
c 100 BC
Marble — height 205 cm
Acquired in 1824
Cardinal Fesch Collection
MA 975

Statuette of pancratiast
1st century AD
Bronze — height 27 cm
Autun
Acquired in 1870
BR 1067

Mercury
Two notches on the head for fixing the wings
Adaptation of the Discophoros of Polyclitus
Second quarter of 1st century AD
Bronze — height 21 cm
Royal Collections
BR 183

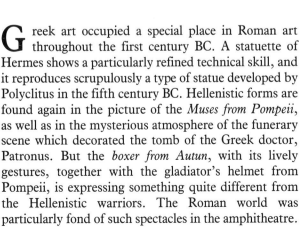

G reek art occupied a special place in Roman art throughout the first century BC. A statuette of Hermes shows a particularly refined technical skill, and it reproduces scrupulously a type of statue developed by Polyclitus in the fifth century BC. Hellenistic forms are found again in the picture of the *Muses from Pompeii*, as well as in the mysterious atmosphere of the funerary scene which decorated the tomb of the Greek doctor, Patronus. But the *boxer from Autun*, with its lively gestures, together with the gladiator's helmet from Pompeii, is expressing something quite different from the Hellenistic warriors. The Roman world was particularly fond of such spectacles in the amphitheatre.

Two Muses : Thalia and Melpomene
Between AD 62 and 79
Wall-painting — height 46 cm
Pompeii
Acquired in 1825 — Gift of Ferdinand IV,
King of Naples, to Napoleon I
Malmaison Collection, then Durand
Collection
P 4

Helmet of Thracian gladiator
1st century AD
Bronze — height 38 cm
Probably Pompeii
Acquired in 1892 — Passed from the
Musée St. Germain
BR 1108

Fragment from the tomb of the doctor, Patronus
Funerary procession
End of 1st century BC
Wall-painting — height 38.7 cm
Rome
Acquired in 1863 — Campana Collection
P 37

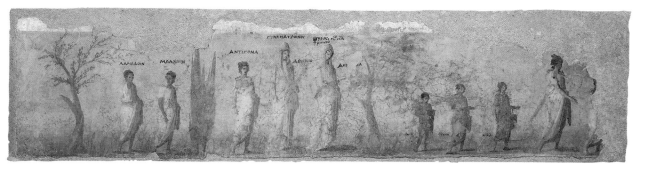

Augustus
Between 27 and 20 BC
Marble — height 26 cm
Cos
Acquired in 1883 — Morellet gift
MA 2577

Livia
c 30 BC
Basalt — height 34 cm
Acquired in 1860 — Fould Collection
MA 1233

Fragment of the Ara Pacis
Erected to celebrate Augustus'
victories in Spain
Between 13 and 9 BC
Marble — height 120 cm
Acquired in 1863
Campana Collection
MA 1088

Claudius
Between AD 41 and 54
Marble — height 32 cm
Thasos (Miller Mission)
Acquired in 1890
MA 1226

Caligula
c AD 31 or 38
Marble — height 47 cm
Thrace
Acquired in 1890
MA 1234

Agrippina the Elder
Between AD 37 and 41
Marble — height 44 cm
Athens
Acquired in 1909
MA 3133

Head of a man
Beginning of 1st century BC
or beginning of 2nd century AD
Bronze — height 22 cm
Acquired in 1865 — Pourtalès Collection
BR 21

Head of a woman
Sometimes identified as Marciana
First quarter of 2nd century AD (?)
Bronze — height 19.4 cm
Acquired in 1848
BR 42

Trajan
After AD 108
Marble — height 200.4 cm
Gabii — acquired in 1808
Borghese Collection
MA 1150

Hadrian
The head belonged to a colossal statue
Second quarter of 2nd century AD
Bronze — height 43 cm
Acquired in 1984
BR 4547

The refined forms of Augustan art harked back to a somewhat academic Classicism. Under Trajan, however, art moved away from such learned works towards more sober expressions of military energy and austerity. The cuirassed statue of the emperor Trajan exalts the power of Rome, just as does his Column celebrating the victory of the legions over the Dacians. This simplicity is like the manner of Republican works, to the point that the dating of certain objects is in doubt, such as the male bronze head which is sometimes thought to be of the first century BC and sometimes of the reign of Trajan. The emperor Hadrian favoured the image of prosperity rather than the image of power. The colossal bronze portrait of him links his majesty with a return to Hellenism, symbolized by the wearing of a beard.

Mosaic pavement
The judgement of Paris
Shortly after AD 115
Marble, limestone and glass
Height 186 cm
Antioch, in the House of the Atrium
Acquired in 1936
MA 3443

Allegorical relief
Personification of the Earth-Mother
Beginning of 2nd century AD
Marble — height 79 cm
Carthage
Acquired in 1856
MA 1838

Herodes Atticus
Between AD 161 and 180
Marble — height 62 cm
Probalinthos, in Herodes Atticus' palace
Acquired in 1865 — Pourtalès Collection
MA 1164

Sarcophagus
The legend of Actaeon
c AD 130
Marble — height 99 cm
Near Rome
Acquired in 1808
Borghese Collection
MA 459

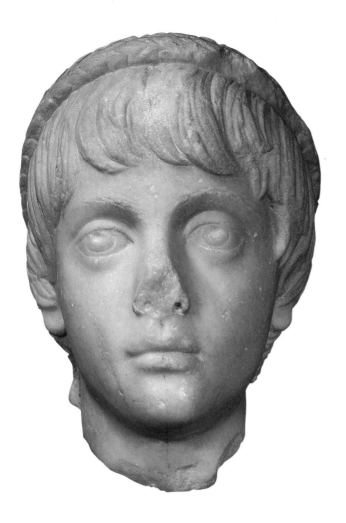

Portrait of a young prince of the Antonine family
Probably one of the nine children of Marcus Aurelius
c AD 170
Marble — height 21 cm
Annaba
Acquired in 1955
MA 3539

T he emperor Hadrian was a philhellene, both by taste and in politics. This is why there was a renaissance of Classicism, which permeated art under his reign, and its influence persisted under his successors, as is shown by the portraits of Herodes Atticus, a wealthy Athenian philosopher who was the friend of Marcus Aurelius, and of an unidentified young Antonine prince. Classicism was now coloured by a touch of almost romantic sensibility, which was achieved by the new practice of drilling the pupils of the eyes to show the statue's gaze. The artists who did this were certainly Greek, like the one who sculpted the *bust of Melitene*, priestess of the Mother of the Gods at the Piraeus. The serious faces of these statues seem to have a presentiment of the dangers of the imminent crisis. The *portrait of Caracalla* shows this most overtly. He has a brutal and perverse look, which seems the opposite of that of the *portrait of Augustus*.

Caracalla
Cuirassed bust
Between AD 212 and 217
Marble — height 50 cm
Acquired in 1815 — Albani Collection
MA 1106

Fragment of a mosaic pavement
Preparations for a banquet
c AD 180-190
Marble, limestone, glass
Height 225 cm
Carthage
Acquired in 1891
MA 1796

Melitene
Priestess of the Mother of the Gods
Consecrated in AD 162
Marble — height 71.5 cm
Piraeus
Acquired in 1914
MA 3068

Plastic vase : bent old woman
She holds a cup in her hand while she dozes
2nd century AD
Bronze — height 9 cm
Vichy
Acquired in 1895
BR 2936

Statuette of Bacchus and Pan
The god of the shepherds hands a grape
to the god of wine
Second half of 2nd century AD
Bronze, incrusted with silver
Height 18.7 cm
Augst
Acquired in 1865
BR 1061

Aphrodite Panthea
The goddess is loaded down with attributes
Roman
Bronze — height 20 cm
Amrith
Acquired in 1868
BR 4425

Plastic vase : bust of a Syrian slave
2nd century AD (?)
Bronze and lead — height 19 cm
Acquired in 1825
Durand Collection
BR 2947

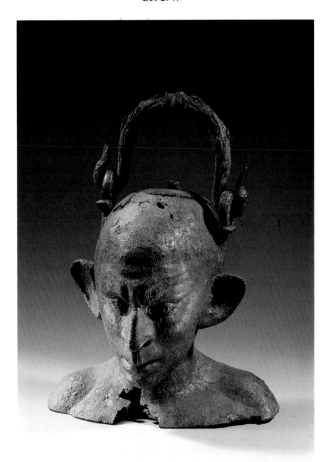

Sarcophagus
Marine procession : marine centaurs,
nereids and cupids
c AD 140-150
Marble — height 95 cm
Church of San Francisco a Ripa (Rome)
Entered the Louvre in 1798; given by
Pius VII to Louis XVIII in 1815.
Albani Collection, then Capitoline Museums
MA 342

Venus, Tritons, Amor and dolphin
The goddess is looking at herself
in a mirror, now missing
4th century AD
Marble — height 76 cm
St. Georges-de-Montagne (Gironde)
Acquired in 1953
MA 3537

Sarcophagus
Dionysus and his band discover Ariadne
on Naxos
Bacchic processions. The unfinished heads
should have been given the features
of the deceased.
Rome workshop, *c* AD 235
Marble — height 98 cm
St. Médard d'Eyrans
Acquired in 1817
MA 1346

Portrait of a charioteer
The head is wearing a chariot-driver's cap
Middle of 3rd century AD
Marble — height 38 cm
MA 341

Sarcophagus
Lion hunt in two scenes
Rome workshop, *c* AD 235-240
Marble — height 88 cm
Acquired in 1808 — Borghese Collection
MA 346

Medallion
Openwork gold sheet, round a coin
of Constantine
Coin struck in AD 321
Gold — diameter 9,2 cm
Acquired in 1973
BJ 2280

Dish
Marine still-life
2nd-3rd century AD
Silver — diameter 34.5 cm
Graincourt-lès-Havrincourt
Acquired in 1959
BJ 2214

Christian sarcophagus
Christ seated and teaching, surrounded by
the Apostles
End of 4th century AD
Marble — height 56 cm
Church of Rignieux-le-Franc
Acquired in 1863
MA 2958

Theodosius II
c AD 440
Marble — height 25 cm
MA 1036

Front part of a head
First half of 3rd century AD
Silver — height 30.5 cm
Notre-Dame-d'Allençon
Acquired in 1852
BJ 2102

Mosaic pavement
Phoenix on a bed of rose-buds
End of 5th century AD
Marble and limestone
Length 600 cm
Antioch, in the courtyard
of a villa at Daphne
Acquired in 1936
MA 3442

Mosaic pavement,
round an octagonal basin
c AD 325-330
Marble, limestone and glass
Together 807 x 804 cm
Antioch, in the Constantinian
Villa at Daphne
Acquired in 1939
MA 3444

Diptych
Six muses and six poets or philosophers
5th century AD
Ivory — height 29 cm
Gaul (?)
Acquired in 1836
SMD 46

Liturgical vessel (?)
Medallions of Christ, St. Peter and
St. Paul, and the Virgin with two angels
End of 6th or beginning of 7th century AD
Silver — height 44 cm
Homs (Syria), ancient Emesa
Acquired in 1892 — Durighello gift
BJ 1895

The earliest period of Christian art is seen in the decoration and furnishings of the churches, illustrated in a panel of mosaic. It interprets the perspective in an individual way : but one can recognize a basilica with three naves and a projecting apse, a plan which belongs with structures of the second half of the fifth century. The raised, silver *vase from Emesa*, which is decorated with medallions enclosing effigies of Christ, Saint Peter and Saint Paul, may have belonged to the liturgical plate from one of these churches, and it was perhaps for the communion wine. But one cannot simply confine early Christian art to the religious evidence. That would be to forget the luxury arts which were current in polite society, such as the leaf from a consular ivory diptych, which was a present given by high officials on special occasions.

Mosaic pavement
Christian basilica
2nd half of 5th
century AD
Marble, limestone,
and perhaps sandstone
and pottery
Length 117.5 cm ;
width 76 cm
Acquired in 1971
De Menil gift
MA 3676

Vase in shape of double head
African red-ware, end of 3rd or
beginning of 4th century AD
Pottery — height 21 cm
Acquired in 1978
CA 6701

Jar
4th century AD
Glass — height 13.6 cm
Banyas (Syria)
Acquired in 1901
MND 486

One of the specific practices of the Christian religion was the cult of relics, and it gave rise to the making of a large number of containers of various shapes and materials, which were for the preservation of the sacred remains. The round-ended precious-metal box from Castell di Brivio is decorated with scenes from the Old and the New Testaments. The same themes are found on marble sarcophagi made in workshops in Rome in the fourth century. Such reliquary boxes must have been placed inside a large stone reliquary. A basalt reliquary from Syria was designed to allow holy oil to be poured onto the sacred relics. The more modest glass cup and pottery vase with two grotesque heads come from the profane world, not the sacred.

Reliquary box
The three Hebrews in the fiery
furnace, the adoration of the Magi
and the resurrection of Lazarus
End of 4th century AD
Gilded silver — height 5.7 cm
Castello di Brivio
Acquired in 1912
BJ 1951

Reliquary in form of a sarcophagus
6th-7th century AD
Basalt — height 89 cm
Syria
Acquired in 1962
MA 3680

Livia as Ceres
c 20 BC
Marble — height 253 cm
Acquired in 1808
Borghese Collection
MA 1242

Credit : Scala Publications Ltd.
Réunion des Musées Nationaux (4, 15hl, 15b, 16hr, 16hl, 17hr,
18l, 18hr, 19, 20l, 21, 22hl, 23h, 24, 25b, 26, 27, 28h, 29h, 30,
33, 34, 35b, 36hl, 37, 38h, 40h, 41, 42, 45l, 46b, 47h, 48l, 49,
50l, 51, 52, 53, 54, 58hr, 58br, 59hr, 60b, 62, 63h, 64h, 65, 66,
71, 72hl, 72hr, 73h, 72-73b, 74r, 74hl, 75, 76hl, 76b, 77r, 79,
81b, 82h, 84, 85h, 86, 87, 88, 89br, 90, 91, 92, 93h, 94b, 95h, 96)

Design : Jérôme Faucheux

Printed in Italy by Graphicom
Colour separations Intégral Graphic
Typesetting Charente Photogravure
Dépôt légal : June 1991